YOU ARE THE FREQUENCY

The Science Behind Alignment, Energy and Manifestation

Loni Maria

Written By Loni Maria
For permissions, contact:
Loni
iloveloni.com
books@iloveloni.com

Cover and interior design by iloveloni

ISBN: 979-8-9932223-8-7
Printed in the United States of America

il♥veloni
www.iloveloni.com

Contents

Introduction

The Shift That Changes Everything:
Why You Don't Attract What You Want — You Align with Who You Are

I used to look at the law of attraction and manifestation as something that was bringing me whatever I wanted and chose to ask for, almost like someone sitting a birthday gift in front of me; and all I had to do was ask, *and that didn't guarantee that I would even get it.* What if I told you that we do not attract what we want, but we align with who we are? It feels like magic, but it's a natural law.

Taking it back to elementary school science where they taught us that everything is energy, whether it is living or not living, and that is only the beginning of what quantum physics has revealed. Everything in our lives — every thought, every emotion, every choice, every outcome — begins with energy. Not the kind of energy we plug into a wall, but the subtle, constant vibration that makes up everything in the Universe. Anything that exist, exists in an energetic field, including us; we are energy. The book you are holding is energy; the chair, bed, or floor you are sitting on is energy. Your thoughts and feelings are energy. The words you speak are energy. Your silence is energy. Your reality - everything you see each day -is energy. Anything that exist is energy! The idea that "everything is energy" might sound broad — but it's not just a belief, it's an invisible intelligence. We live in a Universe that is not random, but responsive. Quantum physics proves that everything in the Universe, from atoms to thoughts, is made up of vibrating energy, but energy doesn't just exist — it interacts, responds, and resonates. This is how energy begins to shape reality: not through coincidence, but through resonance. Resonance is the natural synchronization or connection of energy —when two frequencies match, they amplify each other. Think of a radio when your searching for a station, when two frequencies do not match there is static; when two frequencies match, you get clear sound, music or whatever is playing on that channel. Energy works the same way. Energy is a constant moving vibration. Those vibrations create frequency, which is simply how fast or slow something vibrates or moves.

For example,

- High vibration/ higher frequency = fast-moving, light, expansive energy (love, joy, gratitude).
- High-frequency emotions → attract more high-frequency experiences.
- Low vibration/lower frequency = slow-moving, dense energy (fear, anger, shame).
- Low-frequency emotions → attract more low-frequency experiences.

In simple terms: Everything connects through a frequency of vibration, which is resonance. Since we are energy, we are emitting our own frequencies and things we experience in our everyday reality is only connecting to that frequency, like a radio. "Like attracts like". This could be a high vibration or a low one. Regardless, what you see in your reality is based on what frequency signal you are putting out. Your energy sets the frequency, and your brain's RAS tunes your awareness to match it. Together, they shape the reality you see.

So, what is RAS?

The Reticular Activating System is a neural network system in the brain that controls attention and focus. One of its purposes is to filter sensory data-helping you to only notice what aligns with your dominant focus. It is the brain's filter for reality. I like to call it our brain's algorithm, because that's exactly what it is.

An algorithm is a set of rules that helps a system reach a result. Think of social media or the internet, it knows which videos, Ads and content to try to recommend to you based on previous content that you have engaged with. It is trying to solve a problem of what you like based on what you spend time on. The brain works in a similar way. It filters your reality based on what you spend the most time thinking, feeling, and believing, also known as the set of rules for the algorithm of your life, your reality. This is why when you want a red car, you start seeing red cars everywhere. The red cars were always there all along, but since you have deemed it as important, your brain wants to help you focus on it, so it will help you tune into all the red cars. This is why if someone is running late because they are looking for their keys. They have looked everywhere and cannot find them, while also walking back and forth past them but not knowing it. That is because the brain is tuned into the dominant emotion of panic, and the emotion of losing the keys, not the keys itself. But as soon as the person calms down and shifts into "Let me look for solutions mode," their RAS becomes more open… and suddenly the keys are obvious.

Just as engineers design algorithms for technology, you design the algorithm of your mind through repetition, emotion, belief, and focus. Your RAS becomes the energetic filter through which you experience life. This isn't about hoping, wishing, or waiting for the Universe to deliver something to you. It's about understanding how reality responds to who you are being. As you continue through these pages, you'll see how science, consciousness, and spirituality are not separate ideas — but parts of the same design. You'll see how to align with the things you want and discover reasons why some things you might have asked for are taking the scenic route to get to you. By the end, you will learn to connect with your inner power, so you can consciously create a life filled with more purpose, more peace, and more abundance. This book will help you release your fears, and trust that everything is always working in your favor, even when it doesn't seem like it. You will have a new perspective of life, and understanding of how to change your thoughts, raise your vibrations, and create the life you truly want to live. You don't attract what you want — you align with who you are. What you discover next will change the way you see yourself, your potential, and your entire life.

Take 3 deep breaths — your reality is about to make sense in a way it never has before.

"Whatever you hold in your mind on a consistent basis is exactly what you will experience in your life."

-Tony Robbins

Chapter 1

Self-concept: The Blueprint to Your Reality: *How Who You Believe You Are Shapes Everything You Experience*

Who do you think you are? No- literally. What do you believe about yourself? This is your self-concept. It's the internal identity you hold — your beliefs about your worth, your abilities, what you can have, what you deserve, what's possible for you, etc. It's not who you say you are, it's who you believe you are on the inside. What does that little voice that nobody can hear say about yourself? Do you love yourself? Do you criticize yourself all the time? Do you encourage yourself and congratulate yourself? Are you mean to yourself? How do you think you look? Do you think you are smart? Do you deserve happiness? What do you deserve? The answers to all these questions, would be examples of who you think you are, your self-concept.

Self-concept is the internal blueprint that your mind and energy follow. Who you believe you are, is what the energies around you will react to. We mentioned earlier that thoughts create vibrational frequencies. Some of the most important thoughts you can have are the ones about yourself, because that is where everything starts, with you. Self-concept doesn't just shape what we do...It shapes what we see, and *how* we see all other things. It acts like an internal set of instructions, silently shaping how you show up, what you expect, what you choose, what you allow, etc. Your life can only progress to the level of the identity you believe is yours.

Self- concept is made of your repeated thoughts, your emotional patterns, the expectations you carry, and the identity you've created over time -these are your dominant thoughts and emotions about yourself. Remember we mentioned the set of rules given to your brain to create a result, like your life's algorithm, your self-concept is a set of rules, and your life is the result.

Your brain's Reticular Activating System (RAS) uses your self-concept as the "rules" for what to show you. If you believe you are always overlooked, the brain will focus on all the moments where you are ignored. If you feel like you don't ever have enough money, the brain will look for all the scenarios where your money is not enough. If you think you can't ever do anything right, then your brain will look for just that, all the things you do wrong. If you feel like good things always happen to you, then your brain will find proof of that, by allowing you to see all the good things that happen to you. If you feel like abundance always comes to you, then your brain will show you more abundance. If you feel that you are healthy, the brain will show you more reasons to feel that way.

Advantages of a Positive Self-Concept	Disadvantages of a Negative Self-Concept
1. Higher confidence.	1. Low confidence.
2. Better decision making.	2. Self-sabotage.
3. Healthier relationships.	3. Distorted perception.
4. Increased resilience.	4. Poor boundaries.
5. Improved mental and emotional well-being.	5. Emotional instability.

6. Opportunities become more noticeable.	6. Lower vibration/Negative resonance.
7. Higher vibration/ Better resonance.	7. Missed opportunities
8. Greater success and achievement.	8. Limited growth.

How is self-concept formed?

Self-concept can come from many different things, the most common is from childhood messaging. What did you believe about yourself growing up as a child. What did the people around you help you to believe about yourself? How did your childhood environment influence what you feel about yourself? This is our very first version of self-concept. Some of us may have grown into adults still believing these same concepts, some people may have changed them. Trauma, success, environment, repeated experiences, etc. -Can affect a person's self-concept.

We usually don't choose our original self-concept; we are shaped into it. Over time our life experiences continue to mold it, reinforcing what we believe about ourselves. Regardless, no matter what caused your self-concept to be what it is today, it can always be changed. It's not ever too late to create a new self-concept for yourself or to improve it. Self-concept does not equal truth, it's only what *you* believe.

Does self-concept influence behavior and the decisions you make?

Absolutely! How you feel about yourself can most definitely influence your behavior and the decisions that you make. It can affect habits that are formed and opportunities that are accepted or rejected. For example, someone with a positive self- concept applies for more opportunities, and someone who's self-concept is negative, might talk themselves out of opportunities. Someone with a positive self-concept will have higher standards for themselves and a better chance of being braver and more confident, and someone with a negative self-concept might live more out of fear and have low confidence. People can only accept as much as they would accept from themselves. Your self-concept helps to set the standard of what you will accept in life. If you are not nice to yourself, it would be easier to accept other people not being nice to you as well, because it would feel normal, it would align with your dominant feelings. Self-concept is the real force behind manifestation. You don't get what you want — you get what matches who you believe you are. Think of self-concept as the operating system of your mind. Everything else — thoughts, emotions, choices, opportunities — runs on whatever system is installed at that time.

Negative Thoughts

Negative thoughts are not something to fight or eliminate — they are feedback. They reveal where your self-concept and emotional state are out of alignment. When you try to force positive thinking without changing how you see yourself, the mind resists, creating more tension rather than clarity. This is why shifting negative thoughts is not about control, suppression, or pretending everything is fine. It's about recognizing the state you're in and improving it. As your self-concept begins to shift and your body feels safer and more regulated, your thoughts naturally soften. The mind simply reflects the identity you are operating from. Change the internal relationship, and the thoughts follow.

5 Everyday Ways to Shift Negative Thoughts

1. **Pause and notice how your body feels**

   If your shoulders are tight, your chest feels heavy, or your stomach feels uneasy, etc., that's often where the thought is coming from. Fixing the thought isn't the first step—softening the body is.

2. **Slow down before you think it through**

   Take a breath, unclench your jaw, put your feet on the floor. A calmer body naturally leads to calmer thoughts.

3. **Remind yourself: "This is a reaction, not the truth"**

   Negative thoughts often show up when your system feels stressed or unsafe—not because something is actually wrong.

4. **Shift your attention to something simple and real**

   Look around the room. Notice sounds, light, or movement. This gently pulls you out of the mental

spiral and back into the present
moment.

5. **Do one small thing that matches
the person you want to be**
Send the email. Drink water. Take a
short walk. Action aligned with who
you're becoming changes thoughts
faster than overthinking ever will.

You don't fight negative thoughts — you
update the identity that produces them. Your
reality doesn't start outside of you — it starts
inside of you. Change the blueprint, and the
entire structure of your life shifts.

In simple terms: How you feel about yourself will be the starting point of how other energies can react to you. It starts with you.

"Change your conception of yourself and you will automatically change the world in which you live."

-Neville Goddard

Chapter 2

The Radio of Your Reality: *Coherence, Resonance, and the Signal You're Sending*

We mentioned that your self-concept—what you believe about yourself—is the blueprint for your reality. Everything begins there. Your self-concept also influences whether you are internally coherent or incoherent. Let me explain.

Coherence is when your thoughts, emotions, and overall energy align with your self-concept. Self-concept sets the identity you believe is yours, but coherence determines whether how you are feeling, actually matches that identity.

- If you affirm, "I can do this," (self-concept), and you feel excited, eager, and confident, that is coherence. Your thoughts and emotions match what you believe about yourself, and you send a clear, consistent signal.

- If you affirm, "Good things always come to me," (self-concept), and feel gratitude, happiness, and openness, that is coherence. Again, your emotions align with your self-concept, creating a clear signal.

Note: If your self-concept is negative and your thoughts and emotions match it, this is still coherence, a negative one. Your emotions align with your self-concept — which sends out a clear but low-quality signal. So, if you believe, "I can't do this." (self-concept), and you feel anxiety and fear, then this match is coherence, and it will send a clear negative signal.

But what happens when your self-concept doesn't match your inner thoughts or emotions? This mismatch is called Dissonance. Dissonance sends out an unclear signal -this unclear signal is what we call incoherence, like tuning into a radio station and only hearing static.

For example:

- You affirm you want a healthy relationship (self-concept), but you feel fear, insecurity, or unworthiness. That inner conflict is called dissonance, and it produces an incoherent, unclear static-filled signal.
- You affirm "I am successful" (self-concept), but you feel doubt, pressure, or frustration. That mismatch is dissonance, and it produces an incoherent, static-filled signal.

- You affirm, "I am handsome" or "I am beautiful" (self-concept), but every time you see your reflection you criticize what you see. That is dissonance, and it creates incoherence and an unclear signal.

Any time your thoughts, self-concept, and emotions don't match, the signal becomes distorted — and that distortion is often why what you may be asking for is taking the scenic route to get to you. Like trying to find a clear radio station and only getting static.

Remember, you don't attract what you want — you align with who you are. And if the signal you're sending is unclear, you'll only align with experiences that match that same unclear signal.

In simple terms: Comparing your inner world to a radio: your self-concept chooses the station, and coherence determines how clearly the station comes through, almost like the strength of your antenna. Are you giving off a clear signal to connect to or static?

When your internal world becomes coherent (your self- concept and emotions match), you send out a clear energetic signal. A clear frequency is what allows you to connect with — or "tune into" — other clear frequencies. This is where resonance begins. As mentioned previously, resonance is when a "like frequency" is amplified by another "like frequency". "Like attracts like". This can include low or high frequencies. Resonance only means matching frequencies — when two signals line up, the connection becomes strong. This explains what you naturally connect with and experience in your everyday reality. Resonance is like what you actually hear on the radio when the station comes through clearly.

For example, you're feeling confident, so you notice opportunities, supportive people, and good ideas. Your inner state "matches" experiences that feel confident. If you focus on "there's never enough," -you match with lack, miss opportunities, and connect with situations that reinforce loss or scarcity. So, while resonance determines what you match with, something else is quietly deciding what you actually notice -your RAS.

Whether you have inner coherence or incoherence, your brain's RAS still must do its job. The RAS's primary biological job is to control levels of alertness to include waking up, going to sleep, switching from a deep sleep, to light sleep, to full alertness. It basically determines how "on" or "off" the brain is.

Millions of sensory signals are sent to the brain every second, and we cannot consciously process all that. So, the RAS is like the security at the door of your VIP brain. It only allows a small percentage of information to come in and reach your consciousness. Its objective is to keep you from being overwhelmed, and to reserve energy, so it filters and prioritizes information based on things like what's important for survival, things that you learned to care about or that have emotional significance, things that you focus on repeatedly, etc. This is why you can tune out background noise until you hear someone call your name or can still read a book in the middle of a noisy room.

The RAS sends signals to parts of the brain's cortex that controls attention. It basically regulates what your prefrontal cortex pays attention to. This is why you notice things you have been thinking about, things that matter to you and things that are tied to strong emotions. These filters change based on your internal state (self- concept and emotions).

The RAS also coordinates the brain's response to motivation or threats. If the information gathered by the RAS signals a threat, it will send that information to the emotions department of the brain, the amygdala, and then the amygdala will trigger the body's fight or flight symptoms.

Fight or flight is the body's survival response. When your brain perceives a threat— real *or* perceived—it shifts your body into protection mode.

The goal is to:

- Keep you alive
- Prepare you to fight, run, or freeze
- Conserve energy for survival

If the amygdala perceives danger — even if incorrectly — it fires. I repeat, even if incorrectly -it fires, which would include false dangers. False dangers can be as simple as being scared or nervous about doing something new, having a conversation, a performance or an important speech. A false danger could be anything that your body is currently deeming as "unsafe", even if nothing is actually threatening you. So basically, if the brain senses danger, it reacts—even when no real threat is present. A raised voice, a critical email, conflict, rejection, silence, or no response can trigger the same response as actual danger, all shaping how we feel and respond in the moment. When the body senses danger, it may respond with fight or flight symptoms, which is emotional dysregulation:

- A racing or pounding heartbeat
- Shallow or rapid breathing
- Tightness in the chest or throat
- Muscle tension (especially shoulders, jaw, or stomach)
- Sweaty palms or sudden warmth
- Restlessness or an urge to move
- Feeling on edge, irritable, or easily startled
- Difficulty focusing or thinking clearly
- A sudden need to escape, defend, or shut down
- Trembling
- Tunnel vision
- Digestive upset (nausea, needing to use the bathroom)

Here's why emotional dysregulation matters for alignment and manifestation. When the body is in fight or flight mode, the nervous system is not focused on growth, creativity, or opportunity—it is focused on survival. In this state, your attention narrows. The RAS prioritizes scanning for threats instead of possibilities, filtering your reality through fear, urgency, or self-protection. Even if your conscious mind wants success, love, or expansion, a dysregulated nervous system will keep signaling "not safe yet," creating resistance without you realizing it.

When your inner world becomes coherent, and emotions are regulated, your signal stabilizes. Your RAS then steps in as your internal guide, bringing the right people, cues, and opportunities into focus while quietly shaping what you notice each day. This is where self-concept becomes crucial. The RAS doesn't respond to what you want—it responds to who you believe you are and whether your nervous system feels safe embodying that identity. If your self-concept says, "I am capable, prepared, and expanding," and your body feels regulated, the RAS begins scanning your environment for information that supports that identity. But if your self-concept says "I want success" while your body is in fight or flight, the RAS will stay alert to risk, pressure, and potential failure instead of opportunity. When you decide to see yourself as a business owner—when that identity becomes part of your self-concept—and your emotions are regulated and aligned, you send out a clear signal for what you resonate with. In response, your RAS shifts your attention. You start noticing conversations about opportunities, recognizing useful resources, spotting ideas that support growth, you experience an introduction at the right time, a message that answers a question, or a chance opportunity that feels surprisingly natural. When you begin to see yourself as someone who handles money with confidence and calm, and your emotions are no longer rooted in scarcity or panic, your signal stabilizes. Your RAS begins drawing your attention to budgeting tools, income opportunities, conversations about investing, and practical financial choices. You start making different decisions—not by force, but by awareness. Money feels less stressful, not because more suddenly appears, but because you're seeing options and pathways that were always there. With clarity, signs of alignment become visible. What once felt invisible becomes relevant, not because the world has changed, but because your internal state has. This is what's commonly called the law of attraction—except you aren't pulling anything toward you. You're revealing what was already there. Your brain is now noticing differently. You are aligned.

In simple terms: Coherence powers your signal, Resonance is the frequency you naturally connect with, and your RAS highlights the important signals *for* you to connect to, filtering out the rest.

"When you change the way you look at things, the things you look at change."
— Wayne Dyer

Chapter 3

The Scenic Route: *Why Your Desires Sometimes Take Longer — and What That's Teaching You*

Manifesting is the process of making something clear or evident in your experience. We are always manifesting — the question is whether we are manifesting what we truly want, or what our current internal signal is broadcasting.

As mentioned previously, coherence is the alignment of your thoughts, emotions and self-concept (your internal world), resonance is what you connect to based on that frequency (your external world), and your RAS is what acts on that signal. Resonance explains why something matches your inner state and is available to you. Your RAS explains how you notice, focus on, interact with it once it is available. You're focused and present, and the work seems to move faster. You meet someone and instantly feel at ease, without knowing why. A conversation feels effortless because both people are on the same wavelength. When you're tense, everything feels harder. When you're rushed, obstacles appear. Resonance only happens when there's a clear match between your internal signal and what shows up externally. Whether that signal is positive or negative, your reality reflects the frequency you're sending out and what your RAS is filtering. This is when Manifesting comes in. Resonance is not manifestation itself, but it's the reason manifestation works. Manifestation is the result, but resonance is the mechanism that makes that result appear. Your self-concept creates your internal signal, coherence makes that signal clear, and resonance determines what that signal connects to in your 3D reality. **You don't manifest what you simply want — you manifest what matches your frequency.** Resonance is the matching process, the energetic "yes" that pulls experiences, people, and opportunities into your reality because they align with the signal you are sending out.

Do you see how you are always manifesting? It's never a question of whether you're manifesting — only what you're manifesting. Your reality mirrors your internal broadcast, and the strongest signal always wins. If you're asking for love but speak negatively about yourself, focus more on what's "wrong" than what you appreciate, or feel disappointment every time you look in the mirror, then the signal you're sending out is not only incoherent — it's broadcasting the opposite of love. And you will resonate and connect with experiences that match a frequency of being unloved. This is one-way desires take the scenic route. The question is: Are you sending out the same frequency as what you're asking to receive? If you want love, you must become a love frequency — and that begins with how you love yourself. You can pour love into others all day, but the signal that shapes your reality is the one going to you, from you, not the one going out to them. If you want success, are you aligning with the frequencies of success by showing confidence in yourself, ready to act and believing you can do it? Are you creating everyday habits of a successful person? Or are you in fear of trying anything new, and want to stick with what you know? These are things to consider when asking for what you want. **"What do I need to do to match the frequency of what I want?"**

Emotion is energy in motion. This signal is stronger than words, which are also vibrations. The stronger signal always wins. Biologically: Emotions activate your whole body. Words are processed mainly in the language centers of the brain.

Emotions activate:

- the amygdala
- the limbic system
- your autonomic nervous system
- your hormones
- your heart rhythm
- your breathing pattern

This means emotion sends a full-body signal, while words send a thought-level signal. A full-body signal is always going to be stronger. So, if you say one thing and feel another, the feeling will overpower what you say.

You say, "I'm confident and I know everything will work out", but inside you feel fear, doubt, and anxiety. Even though the words are positive, the emotion (fear) is the stronger energy.

Your internal signal becomes:

- "I'm scared things won't work out."
- "I don't feel capable."

So, your RAS, your nervous system, and your energetic frequency all tune into the feeling, not the words, and that is the signal your reality responds to.

You say, "I'm open to love", but inside you feel unworthy, insecure, or guarded.

Your words send one signal. Your emotions send the opposite signal. The emotion wins — because it carries more energy.

In simple terms: Words send a message, but emotions send the signal. Emotion carries more energy because your entire nervous system responds to it — and the strongest signal always wins.

Emotion is the strongest part of your internal signal. Words express what you want, but emotions express what you truly believe — and the strongest signal dominates. This is why coherence matters so much. Your self-concept must align with your emotions and thoughts, because it's your emotions that reveal what you really believe, not the words you say. Emotions are powerful signals; they broadcast your current self-concept. In fact, the emotions you feel are a direct reflection of your present self-concept.

Self-Concept vs. Surface Words

Self-concept isn't what you say about yourself. It's the deep, internal identity you truly believe. You can say, "I'm confident," but if your emotions and habitual reactions reflect fear, insecurity, or doubt, then your self-concept isn't actually confident — you are only saying it is. You might say, "I'm ready for this opportunity," but inside you feel anxiety, doubt, and fear of failure. Even though the words are positive, your emotions broadcast the opposite signal. Your self-concept at that moment — what you truly believe about yourself — is reflected in the fear, not the words. As a result, your internal signal is incoherent, and your reality responds to the strongest energy: your emotion, fear. This is another reason why desires may take the scenic route —again, reality responds to the signal being sent, not just what you say you want.

Delays aren't failures — they're safeguards. Your subconscious and brain are designed for survival, and it will only help you get what it believes you can handle -the frequency you are vibrating at. Think of an electronic that needs batteries to operate, they all have a certain amount of voltage that is required for it to operate properly. No more, no less. A lamp, may require a certain bulb or wattage for it to work properly. Even if the bulb fits, if the wattage is not the amount that matches the lamp, the light will not be as bright and could even cause damage or a fire. It is the same with your body; it does not want to start a fire or cause damage so it will meet you where you are. If you believe you can only carry 50lbs, your brain does not want to point you towards 500lbs, makes sense? Basically, delays often happen because your brain doesn't yet perceive your desire as safe. Your nervous system prioritizes protection, so until your thoughts, emotions, and self-concept signal that what you want and are asking for is secure and manageable, manifestation may take the scenic route. Figure out what it is that you want and start acting as if you have it already or do small things that align with it. The mind does not know the difference on rather you have it or not, only the emotions and the habits of it. Once it deems these habits and emotions as important, your RAS will help you focus on more things that align with that path. Feel the way you would feel if you had what you are asking for. Would you be sad, frustrated or happy with what you are asking for? If you would be happy then you should try to be happy and positive as much as you can to be able to connect with things on that frequency.

You have to feel and be on the frequency of what you are asking for. This allows for more connection versus the scenic route.

From a broader perspective, you can have anything you ask for. On a quantum level, every possibility already exists simultaneously, you just have to tap into the frequency of it. Different outcomes, experiences, and versions of life coexist all at the same time—not because they are being created from nothing, but because they already exist. Since everything is energy, all possibilities exist at once. What determines which one you experience is not effort or force, but alignment. When your inner state changes, you don't create a new reality—you simply tune into a different one. Just like a radio doesn't make music, it receives the station it's tuned to. When you want to hear a different station, you don't create a new one—you turn the dial to match a new frequency. Your frequency determines which possibilities become real for you, a match.

Note: Don't be discouraged, sometimes alignment can take time. At the same time, timing isn't a limitation; you can manifest things quickly—even the same day—depending on what you're asking for and how long it takes to align your inner state with what you desire. Basically, how prepared are you to receive what you are asking for? Is it safe?

"You become what you believe, not what you think or what you want."

-Oprah Winfrey

Chapter 4

The Intelligence You're Already Aligned With

Spirituality is the practice of connecting with the energy that flows through everything — yourself, others, and the world around you; the answer for it all. It brings awareness and understanding of the unseen forces that guide your life, trusting your intuition, and understanding that your inner energy shapes your experiences. Spirituality helps you uncover your purpose, release what no longer serves you, and align with the life you truly desire. It's about growth, recognizing the power you have within to influence your 3D reality, and the connection to something greater than you, such as God, The Universe, a higher power or the energy flow of life.

47

Spirituality can be expressed through religion, meditation, art, prayer and many other ways.

How does spirituality affect your 3D reality?

Spirituality helps you open the door to purpose, growth, and the life you truly desire. When you're not aware of the invisible intelligence that underlies everything — the energy, intuition, and guidance always available to you — you end up manifesting on autopilot, operating from your default inner frequency. Spirituality helps you move out of that unconscious mode. It strengthens your connection to your intuition, heightens your awareness of the signals your mind and body are always sending, and deepens your understanding of your own thoughts and emotions.

For example, you might say you want success, but if you are not spiritually in tuned with yourself or the spiritual source around you, then you might miss opportunities that are right in front of you. This awareness matters, because the way you think and feel is what shapes the energy you broadcast — again, that energy determines the reality you experience. This is where spirituality opens the door for consciousness.

Consciousness is simply being aware. The ability to notice your thoughts, emotions, and experiences. Spirituality is the practice of expanding that awareness. When you are able to be aware of your thoughts and feelings, this allows you to monitor them closely and make changes when you need to.

If you realize you are thinking negatively, you have the opportunity to change it. When you are not aware of your feelings, thinking negatively can go unnoticed and unchanged, also affecting your everyday life. Whether you are aware of your thoughts and feelings or not, resonance will still happen, and you will connect with the frequency you're sending out. Spirituality, the connection to the higher source is what helps you stay guided, centered, and aligned with the reality you want to create.

In simple terms: Spirituality is the awareness that you are connected to something bigger than yourself — and learning how to work with that connection.

Ways to practice spirituality:

Spirituality can be practiced in many ways, and you can always choose the method that works best for you. **Don't be afraid to try something new because it can be hard to open new doors with the same old keys.**

Quiet moments of stillness- even a few quiet moments a day can help you reconnect with yourself, calm your mind and hear your intuition more clearly.

Any style of meditation- you can focus on your breathing, sit in silence, pray, listen to guided meditations or tunes and sound waves.

Gratitude- writing or thinking about things you are grateful for shifts your vibration and opens you up to receiving. When you are giving energy to all the things that makes you happy and that you are grateful for, your RAS will show you more of it.

Journaling- writing out your thoughts, feelings and desires help you see your inner world more clearly.

There are many other ways to become more spiritual -the method does not matter, the awareness does.

"What you seek, is seeking you."

-Rumi

Chapter 5

Habits: *Identity in Motion*

Habits are the actions, thoughts, and emotional responses you repeat more of—often without realizing it. They are the automatic behaviors your brain performs on your behalf so it can save energy. Remember, the brain is designed for survival, and conserving energy. The brain loves patterns, and habits removes the extra step of the decision-making process. The brain would prefer to function through habits versus creating something new every single time, it is more efficient. Almost like setting your alarm clock to automatically repeat daily, rather than having to remember to set it every single day, it's more efficient.

Although the brain would prefer to use a habit first before creating something new, not all habits are beneficial. Some habits hurt rather than help. Habits are not there because they are positive or negative, habits are only there because it is something that you have grown used to doing repeatedly and it is now a natural occurrence in your life. It can take anywhere from 16 to over 200 days to create a habit. Imagine the habits you have been relying on your entire life. There are different types of habits that you experience.

Examples:

Thought Habits

- Assuming the worst
- Overthinking
- Imagining success
- Practicing gratitude

Emotional Habits

- Defaulting to anxiety
- Reacting with anger
- Feeling excited about possibilities
- Trusting yourself

Behavioral Habits

- Procrastinating
- Journaling
- Scrolling mindlessly
- Taking small consistent actions towards goals

Your habits become you, and they help determine your identity. Habits are the patterns that train your mind, energy and RAS to repeat the same results. If your daily habits don't match the identity you want, you will continue to live the same story, even if you want something new. When your habits align with your desired self, your entire system becomes coherent and then change becomes a natural instinct and not forced.

We tend to stick to habits that match who we believe we are. When something doesn't align with our self-concept, the brain may resist it because it feels unfamiliar or unsafe to the nervous system.

For Example: The Gym Person vs. The "I'm Not Athletic" Person.

- If someone sees themselves as a healthy athletic person, then going to the gym regularly will feel like a natural habit. (The habit matches their identity)
- If someone sees themselves as lazy or "I'm not athletic", the brain resists that same exact habit, not because it is hard, but because it conflicts with

who they believe they are. (So, it will feel forced)

For Example: Money Habits

-If someone believes "I am good with money", then budgeting, saving and investing money will feel more aligned.

-If someone believes "I am always broke", then their brain will subconsciously resist budgeting habits because it does not align with who they believe they are.

In Simple Terms: Habits do not stick because of willpower; they stick because of identity. Your brain is wired to behave like the person you believe you are. When a habit matches who you believe you are it will feel natural. When it doesn't, your mind will resist it, even if it is good for you. **So, habits are not just routines, they are reflections of who we believe we are.**

Again, your self-concept (who you believe you are) is your internal blueprint. Coherence aligns your thoughts, emotions and energy. Resonance amplifies the signal with connection, and your RAS filters your reality to match it (what you see every day). Your habits are the action expression of who you believe yourself to be.

Your brain prefers consistency. If you believe, "I am a confident person", then your habits will reflect confidence. If you believe, "I'm always overwhelmed", then your habits will reflect overwhelm.

Identity $\rightarrow$ Thoughts $\rightarrow$ Emotions $\rightarrow$
Actions $\rightarrow$ Results $\rightarrow$ Reinforces Identity.

*This loop is the foundation of why habits stick. Your identity creates thoughts, thoughts create emotions, emotions lead to actions, actions bring results, those results reinforce your identity.

Your self-concept is the internal story, and your habits are the daily proof of that story. A fit person works out because it's who they are, not because they have to. A messy person struggles to stay organized even with planners and apps. A successful person naturally seeks solutions instead of problems. **Your brain wants you to act like you, the you, it believes you are.**

Manifestation is not magic, it's alignment. What you repeatedly do becomes the life you repeatedly experience. **Your habits are the daily vote to the reality you are creating.**

We now understand that habits are closely tied to self-concept—who we believe we are. While it's possible to force new behaviors through discipline alone, they often require constant effort to maintain.

Lasting change tends to happen when habits align with identity. Rather than focusing only on what you want to do, consider who you're becoming. As your sense of self shifts, your habits begin to feel more natural, and consistency requires less effort.

Instead of saying you want to meditate, say "I am someone who stays grounded and calm".

Instead of "I want to save money", say "I am someone who manages money confidently".

"I am – (insert whoever you choose to be)" Once you have secured the identity, choose small habits that align with it, so small that it is very easy to do.

For example:

Identity: I am a healthy person.

Small habit: Drink one glass of water when you wake up.

Identity: I am a productive person.

Small habit: Do something productive 3 minutes a day.

Once again, the brain loves consistency. Small wins build trust with yourself and also become a habit with time. Small habits help create coherence.

Next, attach the habit to something you already do, it helps to make the habit automatic.

For example:

- after you get in the car, say your affirmations.
- After you brush your teeth, write down or say all the things you are grateful for.
- After making your morning coffee, review your goals.

Current routine- Attach new habit. Since the brain loves patterns, this will make the habit easier to remember and repeat.

Next, you have to remove any friction by making your new habit easier and possible to do, and the old habit harder to do.

For example:

- You want to work out, lay your clothes out the day before.
- You want to read more, put a book on your pillow or on the nightstand.
- You want to stop scrolling, keep your phone across the room unless it's important.

*The easier the behavior, the faster it becomes automatic.

After you have made it easier to complete your small habit, you must now create coherence, by aligning your emotions. An example of where people fail: your intention says, "I want to work out", but your emotions say, "I dread working out". Your body is incoherent and the habit won't stick. In order to create coherence, remind yourself why this habit matters, visualize the version of you that successfully does the habit, and feel gratitude as if the habit is already yours; feel happy to complete the habit.

You must repeat this entire process until your RAS accepts the behavior as "important".

Repetition+ Emotion= Priority

Once your RAS believes this habit is a part of who you are, it will become automatic. Your brain will notice opportunities to help you do the habit, it will help make it feel natural and filter out distractions that interrupt it. This is when the habit becomes effortless.

Finally, you must celebrate yourself every time you complete the habit no matter how small. Celebration tells the brain, "This behavior matters, do it again!" It also releases dopamine, a brain chemical released to influence feelings of pleasure, motivation and reinforcement. It helps the brain know what to do more of. You can celebrate with a smile, saying, "yes" in your mind, gratitude for staying consistent, checking it off of a list, or you can celebrate big; but celebrate.

Let the small habits pile up into identity. Small habits equal consistency, consistency equals identity, identity equals big habits, big habits equal a new reality! This is how transformation happens.

Don't Give Up

Change can feel discouraging at times. You may be trying to shift a habit or manifest something new, and it can seem like nothing is working. This is the moment when giving up feels tempting—but it's also the moment when persistence matters most.

Real change can take time. Again, research suggests it can take over 200 days to form a new habit, especially when you're undoing patterns you've carried for years, it depends on the person. Your body and nervous system need time to adjust to what's unfamiliar. That doesn't mean you're failing—it means you're learning. Think of a child, when they are learning something new, they make mistakes, but as they continue to do the task and grow they get the hang of it. Creating a new habit is like a child learning something new.

At first, the new habit may feel uncomfortable or difficult. That's normal. Doing something new can feel hard because it challenges your existing self-concept and automatic responses. This is where self-motivation, awareness, and spirituality come in—the willingness to stay present and keep choosing alignment, even when it's uncomfortable.

You don't have to be perfect. You will stumble. What matters is that you continue. It's okay to fall short—but it's not okay to stay there. Every time you return to the practice, you reinforce who you are becoming and make sure to celebrate that win.

Remember, repetition is what helps the brain learn, so stay positive and keep going. It does get easier. And one day, what once felt hard will feel natural.

In Simple Terms:

1. Choose an identity.
2. Pick a small habit that matches it.
3. Stack it onto to something you already do.
4. Remove friction (make the new habit easy and the old habit hard)
5. Create emotional coherence. (feel happy about the habit)
6. Repeat until your RAS takes over.
7. Celebrate the behavior.
8. Let the identity shift takeover.

*When your identity matches the habit, the habit becomes effortless.

"The mind is everything. What you think, you become."

-Buddha

Chapter 6

Reprogramming the Subconscious:

Practices That Connect Desire and Belief

Now we know what a habit is and how it really is a summary of who we believe we are. Now, although habits are automatic, they can still be negative automatic actions, or positive automatic actions. Is it automatic for you to think the worst in situations -or the best? Is it automatic for you to believe you can complete something new -or do you doubt yourself? Is it automatic for you to resist change -or adapt with ease? These are patterns worth paying attention to. The actions, thoughts and reactions you repeat everyday reveal your self-concept. Ask yourself, "Do my automatic behaviors align with the version of me I'm trying to become, the things I say I want?"

This is for you to determine and notice. Do the things you spend most of your time doing every day align with who you want to be, or the things that you ask for?

Your conscious mind is the part of you that thinks, analyzes, decides and chooses what you want. Your subconscious mind is the part of you that automatically run your beliefs, habits, emotions and reactions. Your conscious mind speaks the language of choice, and your subconscious speaks the language of repetition. Think of your subconscious mind like the operating system, and your conscious mind is like the programmer of the system. The conscious mind has to speak a language that the system understands. The subconscious does not change through logic or willpower, it changes through repetition, emotion, imagery and experience. The subconscious mind is like our body's autopilot. It memorizes and learns by patterns and stores the patterns along with learned behaviors. It responds more to emotions than words. Your conscious mind learns from awareness (noticing your thoughts, emotions and habits), logic and reasoning (thinking, analyzing, questioning and making decisions), intention (deciding what you want), choice and focus. Whatever the conscious mind focuses on becomes the "instruction" sent to the subconscious mind.

In Simple Terms:

The conscious mind learns by what you focus on. The subconscious mind learns by what you repeat.

Once you become aware of the habits that shape your identity, the next step is to choose new patterns that support the version of you that you are becoming; and get rid of the ones that don't. This is where intentional practices come in. Habits don't just change because we want them to, they change because we repeatedly give our mind and body a new experience, a new pattern to normalize. With this awareness in place, the next step is to put it into action through practices that align your conscious choices with your subconscious patterns.

This is where consciousness plays its part. Practices like meditation, journaling, visualization, gratitude, embodiment, vision boards and detachment, are not just spiritual tools -they are consciousness tools. They bridge the gap between what you want and what your subconscious believes. Each one communicates something different to the subconscious, while also helping with manifesting and alignment -let's break it down.

Meditation

Meditation is more than just sitting still -it's training your mind to return to clarity, the practice of intentionally focusing your mind. There are many forms of meditation, a popular one is breath awareness.

Powerful Benefits:

- Teaches the mind to slow down and observe without reacting.

- Helps to calm the nervous system - reduces stress by lowering cortisol levels, helps your body shift out of fight-or-flight mode and into a regulated state. (This help with coherence and making sure you are sending out a clear signal)

- Increases self-awareness by helping you to notice your thoughts, instead of being controlled by them. Helps you see the patterns, reactions and beliefs that are shaping your reality. (awareness allows you to notice when changes need to be made)

- Help you rewrite your subconscious. When the mind becomes quiet, the subconscious becomes more open and receptive. This allows you to plant new beliefs, new stories, and new self-concepts.

- Strengthens your focus and attention by training your conscious to stay focused on what matters, this also helps to improve what the RAS filters in your reality and what to focus on.

- Improves emotional regulation and reduces reactivity, helping you make choices from your higher self instead of old wounds.

- Enhances coherence. By aligning your thoughts, energy and emotions, it is creating internal coherence - sending a clearer and stronger signal for manifestation (alignment).

- Raises your vibrations. Slower breathing, calmer thoughts and clarity naturally shifts your frequency upward. Higher vibrations and emotions like peace, gratitude, and clarity become your natural state.

- Reduces overthinking. Meditation interrupts the worry and fear. You gain a space between you and your thoughts, giving you room to replace them with new ones.

- Improves sleep and mental clarity. A less cluttered mind leads to deeper rest, better problem solving and sharper intuition.

- Strengthens mind-body connection. By turning inward, you become more aware of physical tension and emotional cues.

- Supports identity shifts. Meditation helps you detach from old versions of yourself and step into a new self-concept. It is easier to become someone new when you create mental space for that change.

- Helps you respond instead of reacting. Meditation creates a pause between stimulus and response. The pause is where your power lives -and new habits are formed.

Visualization

Visualization is more than imagination -it's mental rehearsal for your future, and also another form of meditation. It trains your brain to recognize opportunities, builds the emotional state of already having what you want, and trains your mind to treat your desires as familiar instead of distant.

Powerful Benefits:

- Programs the subconscious mind. Visualization gives your mind a new pattern to accept as normal. The subconscious does not distinguish between real and fake experiences -it simply stores whatever is repeated. (This makes your desired identity or outcome feel familiar instead of foreign)

- Activates the RAS. When you vividly visualize what you want, your RAS treats it as important. This causes your brain to look for opportunities, notice resources, and filter information that aligns with your goals. Visualization trains your brain to see what matches your vision.

- Strengthens internal coherence. When you see your future in your mind, it helps to align your emotions, thoughts and intentions -creating coherence, which strengthens manifestations (alignment).

- Building confidence and belief. Visualizing success repeatedly creates a feeling of "I can do this". You begin acting like the person who achieves those outcomes because the experience already feels real.

- Rehearses the future. Visualizing is a mental practice that athletes, performers and leaders use to mentally rehearse before taking action. This smooths out fear and increases competence.

- Raises emotional frequency. When you imagine the life you want, you naturally create the emotions of joy, gratitude, excitement, and possibility. These emotions raise your vibrations and shift your self-concept upwards.

- Reduces fear and anxiety. When you visualize a positive outcome, it calms the brain's threat system, helping you shift from survival mode to expansion mode -creating emotional safety for change.

- Makes habits easier to adopt. When the brain has already seen and felt the future version of you, the habits that match that version feel more natural and less forced.

- Clarifies your goals. Visualization helps you become specific, get clear on what you want, understand how you want to feel, and define the identity you want to step into. Clarity creates alignment.

- Supports manifestation. Visualization is the bridge between the internal and the external world. You see it internally first -you tune into it emotionally -your RAS filters for it - you take aligned action -your reality shifts.

- Strengthens neural pathways. Repeated visualizations build the same neural circuits that physical action builds. Your brain becomes wired for success before you ever take a step.

- Changes your self-concept. When you repeatedly see yourself as confident, successful, capable, abundant, or loved, your subconscious begins to accept that identity as truth.

Gratitude

Gratitude is more than feeling thankful -it's a frequency shift. It changes your emotional baseline, your chemistry and the way your brain filters reality. Gratitude trains your energy and mind to look for abundance instead of lack.

Powerful Benefits:

- Raises your emotional frequency. Gratitude is a high vibration state. (similar to joy, love and appreciation). It immediately shifts you out of fear, frustration and scarcity -and into openness, connection and possibility.

- Retrains your RAS. When you consistently practice gratitude, your RAS starts to notice opportunities, support, solutions, good moments and progress -things to be grateful for instead of problems and worst-case scenarios.

- Rewires the subconscious. Gratitude teaches your subconscious "Good things happen to me. I am supported. Life works in my favor." Over time this becomes your default identity, not just a practice.

- Builds internal coherence. Feeling gratitude aligns your thoughts, emotions and nervous system. It pulls your mind and body into a unified state, making your signal clearer - which strengthens resonance. (needed for manifesting/alignment)

- Reduces stress and overthinking. People who practice gratitude bounce back faster from setbacks. It trains the mind to zoom out and see the bigger picture instead of collapsing it into a negative moment. -helping you to find the positive in any negative.

- Reinforces a positive self-concept. Gratitude helps you to see how far you have come, what you have survived, what you have achieved, what you already have. This strengthens your self-worth and rewrites old internal narratives.

- Amplifies manifestation. Gratitude sends a strong signal of "I have" instead of "I lack", which boost resonance, raises your vibration, and aligns you with more of the same frequency. It magnetizes experiences that match the emotional state you are practicing.

Journaling

Journaling is more than just writing on paper -it's a tool that brings the unseen into the physical world. It gives form to thoughts, emotions, desires and patterns that usually stay unconscious. Writing is a bridge between your inner world and outer reality. Statistics also shows that writing down your goals can increase your chances of achieving them by 42%. (More people accomplish their goals when they are written down versus just saying them) There are many different methods of journaling. From goals, to gratitude, scripting, affirmations and more.

Powerful Benefits:

- Clears mental clutter. Journaling helps you release what's stuck in your mind. When you write your thoughts out, the mind no longer needs to hold them. This creates space for clarity, intuition and new ideas.

- Makes the subconscious visible. Most of what shapes your reality comes from your subconscious. Through journaling, hidden beliefs, fears and patterns rise to the surface where you can finally work with them to make changes.

- Strengthens manifestation. Writing activates clarity, direction and energetic direction. When you put a desire or goal in writing, you're giving it structure. It becomes more real, more focused, and easier for the mind and energy to align with it.

- Reprograms the RAS. Journaling about goals, gratitude, or identity sends consistent instructions to your RAS. Your brains begin to notice opportunities, synchronies, solutions, and evidence that supports what you are writing. It trains your mind what to focus on.

- Reduces stress and emotional pressure. Putting emotions into words is a powerful release. It lowers nervous system activation and helps you process experiences without suppressing them.

- Helps you understand yourself. Journaling creates self- awareness. It shows you what you truly want, what drains you, what patterns repeat, what still needs healing, what you've outgrown. It creates the self- honesty needed for growth.

- Tracks your spiritual and personal evolution. When you look back you can see how much you've healed, transformed and manifested. It becomes evidence of your progress and a reminder of your strength.

- Strengthens intuition. Writing allows you to bypass the analytical mind. As you journal, intuitive messages, ideas and inner guidance surfaces naturally.

- Improves emotional regulation. By expressing thoughts and feelings through writing, you build emotional intelligence and learn to respond and not react.

- Deepen your relationship with yourself. The more you write, the more connected you become with your inner voice.

Vision Board

A vision board is a visual command to your mind -it tells your brain what to notice, your energy what to feel, and your identity what to grow into. It is a collection of images and/or words put into a collage to represent your goals and desires. It can be physical or digital.

Powerful Benefits:

- Clarifies your desires. Turning vague goals into clear images gives your mind something specific to target.

- Activate the RAS: Visual cues tell your Reticular Activating System what to filter for and what opportunities to notice.

- Increase motivation. Seeing your goals daily strengthens emotional connection and drive.

- Reinforce identity. The images you choose reflect the version of yourself that you are becoming, helping your subconscious internalize it.

- Strengthens visualization. Vision boards make mental imagery easier, bridging imagination and physical reality.

- Create emotional alignment. Looking at the board creates feelings of you already having what you want, which strengthens coherence and resonance.

Embodiment

Embodiment is the practice of physically acting as the version of yourself you intend to become, teaching your subconscious to believe it's real through action, posture, behavior and state. "Acting as if."

Powerful Benefits:

- Programs the subconscious through action. Your body sends signals to your mind; when you behave like your desired identity, your subconscious begins to accept it as truth.

- Creates coherence between thoughts, emotions and behavior. You're not just thinking differently, you're showing up differently.

- Builds confidence through repetition: Repeatedly acting as your future self, strengthens a new automatic way of being.

- Improves emotional regulation. Embodying calm, empowered or confident states teaches your nervous system new baselines.

- Strengthens manifestation: Acting "as if", makes your internal state match your desired reality, increasing resonance.

- Breaks old patterns. When your behavior changes, old habits lose power and new ones become natural.

- Reinforces self-concept. Embodiment is self-concept in motion. It makes identity shift physical, not just mental.

Detachment

Detachment isn't about "not caring" -it's about releasing the fear, pressure, and control that blocks what you're trying to create. It shifts you from force to flow.

Powerful Benefits:

- Reduces mental pressure. When you stop obsessing over the outcome, your nervous system relaxes -making clarity, creativity and intuition stronger.

- Breaks the cycle of resistance. Clinging to an outcome creates tension ("Why isn't it here yet?"). Tension sends an unclear signal. Detachment dissolves that tension - allowing things to unfold more naturally.

- Strengthens self-trust. Letting go strengthens the belief that you can handle anything -increasing confidence and emotional stability.

- Improves manifestation/alignment. When you're no longer gripping the desire with fear and neediness, your energy becomes clearer, cleaner and more magnetic.

- Supports healthy decision making. Detachment removes desperation, so choices come from clarity, instead of panic or insecurity.

- Opens space for better outcomes. Sometimes what you want is limited compared to what's possible. Detachment allows life to give you the upgraded version.

As you practice reprogramming the subconscious, remember that repetition creates familiarity, and familiarity creates safety. You are not trying to force change— you are allowing your mind and body to learn a new way of being. Each visualization, affirmation, moment of gratitude, and pause of presence is a signal to your subconscious that this new reality is possible and safe. Over time, these practices become less like techniques and more like a natural state of alignment. When belief begins to feel embodied rather than imagined, your outer world responds effortlessly. You are no longer chasing the outcome—you are becoming the version of yourself who naturally receives it.

"It's your road, and yours alone. Others may walk it with you, but no one can walk it for you."

-Rumi

Chapter 7

From Blocks to Flow: Returning to Coherence

Common Manifestation Blocks

- Fear
- Doubt
- Incoherence
- Attachment
- Identity Conflict

Emotional regulation is the *bridge* between knowing and doing. It is what allows your nervous system, subconscious mind, and new identity to align with each other instead of competing.

When emotions are dysregulated:

- The RAS filters for danger instead of opportunity
- The subconscious stays stuck in survival patterns
- Coherence collapses
- Old identity wins
- Manifestation becomes "blocked"

When emotions are regulated:

- The RAS opens and becomes receptive
- The brain can integrate new patterns
- The body stops sending mixed signals
- Change feels safe
- The new identity becomes possible

Regulating your emotional state is one of the most powerful tools for manifestation and alignment. It clears interference, aligns your energy, and frees your subconscious to support your desires. Think of a radio, if your emotional frequency is all over the place, up and down and not regulated, it will send a static-filled unclear signal, making it hard to connect to. When the emotions are clear and regulated and flowing smooth, it sends a clear signal, causing clear results.

How To Regulate in The Moment

1. Reassure Yourself

When your emotions are dysregulated, immediately tell yourself, "I am okay, I am safe", even if you do not fully believe it. Your nervous system responds to the tone and intention. Keep repeating as often as needed.

2. Breathe Deeply

Stop what you are doing and take as many slow, deep breaths as you can (You can start with 3 at a time and keep going until the body starts to settle). Breathing signals safety. It resets the nervous system faster than anything else. Keep repeating as often as needed.

3. Redirect Your Mind

If possible, write down:

- A few things you're grateful for
- Something positive that grounds you or makes you feel positive
- Or a simple calming statement like: "This feeling is temporary. I am returning to peace."

You can also journal the emotion itself, reminding yourself that it's only passing through — not defining you and not stopping your manifestation.

Anything outside of peace, clarity, or joy, is a moment of dysregulation -not a failure or a setback. This includes anxiety, sadness, being upset or frustrated. Recognize the feeling, soothe it, and allow the old emotion to move out of your system instead of resisting it. It is also okay to feel down or to have bad days, give yourself a time frame like 3 minutes or 3 days, however long you need to sit with your emotions before you have to force yourself to get back to your regulated higher frequency.

This is not you trying to force yourself to be happy, this is you shifting your body out of survival mode.

Even when you understand the principles of manifestation, you may still find yourself feeling stuck. This doesn't mean you're doing anything wrong — it simply means your mind and body are sending mixed signals, creating interference between the version of you who wants the desire and the version of you who is used to the old reality.

These blocks are normal, and every person experiences them at some point on their manifestation journey and in life. Becoming aware of them is what helps you shift out of resistance and back into alignment.

Manifestation is not about perfection — it's about alignment.

Your emotions are not the enemy. They are signals. When you learn to calm and regulate your internal world, your outer world responds effortlessly. The more safety you create inside yourself, the easier it becomes for your new identity, new beliefs, and new reality to take root.

You are not blocked — you are simply learning how to get back into coherence. And with practice and patience, this becomes more natural. Once coherence is restored, your inner state begins to guide your experience in very practical ways.

Imagine you see yourself as someone worthy of a healthy, secure relationship (self-concept), and your emotions reflect that belief—you feel calm, open, and grounded (coherence). That inner alignment sends out a clear signal.

Because of that signal, you naturally resonate with people and situations that feel safe, mutual, and emotionally available. You're drawn to conversations that feel easy, not forced, and to people who meet you with respect.

At the same time, your RAS is filtering your experience. You notice green flags more quickly -consistent communication, emotional presence, shared values—and you're less pulled toward chaos or mixed signals. Nothing magical appeared overnight. Love didn't suddenly arrive. You simply became aligned enough to notice what was already there. When your inner world is coherent, resonance draws the connection, and your RAS helps you recognize it.

This is how coherence, resonance, and the RAS work together in everyday life. Nothing is forced; nothing is chased. As your inner world becomes aligned, what you connect with naturally changes. The work isn't about controlling reality—it's about becoming clear enough to recognize what already belongs to you.

Conclusion

In the end, every technique you've learned—all points back to one truth: your life responds to who you believe you are. You are not trying to attract a new reality; you are becoming the version of yourself who naturally lives it. Change doesn't happen through force, luck, or waiting for the Universe to choose you. It happens through alignment, repetition, awareness, and identity. You are not just observing your life—you are actively shaping it. You are the creator, the observer, and the main character.

"If one advances confidently in the direction of his dreams, and endeavors to live the life which he has imagined, he will meet with a success unexpected in common hours."

— *Henry David Thoreau*

About The Author

Loni Maria is a writer, entrepreneur and creative who explores the relationship between awareness, alignment, and the way life unfolds. Her work blends reflective insight with grounded understanding, offering a calm and accessible approach to topics often viewed as complex or abstract.

Through her writing, Loni invites readers to look beyond effort and control and instead explore the subtle shifts that shape everyday experience. Her work is rooted in curiosity, lived experience, and a deep appreciation for the unseen forces that influence how we perceive and engage with the world. This is one of the things that has changed her life, and she wishes the same for you.